LET US DANCE

A **devotional** and guided
journal for **growing** in grief

This Journal
Belongs To:

Lamentations 3

1 I am the man who has seen affliction
  by the rod of the Lord's wrath.
2 He has driven me away and made me
  walk in darkness rather than light;
3 indeed, he has turned his hand against
  me again and again, all day long.

4 He has made my skin and my flesh grow
  old and has broken my bones.
5 He has besieged me and surrounded
  me with bitterness and hardship.
6 He has made me dwell in darkness
  like those long dead.

7 He has walled me in so I cannot escape;
  he has weighed me down with chains.
8 Even when I call out or cry for help,
  he shuts out my prayer.
9 He has barred my way with blocks of
  stone; he has made my paths crooked.

10 Like a bear lying in wait, like a lion in
  hiding,
11 he dragged me from the path and
  mangled me and left me without help.
12 He drew his bow and made me the
  target for his arrows.

13 He pierced my heart with arrows from
  his quiver.

14 I became the laughingstock of all my
  people; they mock me in song all day
  long.
15 He has filled me with bitter herbs and
  given me gall to drink.

16 He has broken my teeth with gravel;
  he has trampled me in the dust.

17 I have been deprived of peace;
  I have forgotten what prosperity is.
18 So I say, "My splendor is gone
  and all that I had hoped from the
  Lord."

19 I remember my affliction and my
  wandering, the bitterness and the gall.
20 I well remember them, and my soul is
  downcast within me.
21 Yet this I call to mind and therefore I
  have hope:

22 Because of the Lord's great love we are
  not consumed, for his compassions
  never fail.
23 They are new every morning; great is
  your faithfulness.
24 I say to myself, "The Lord is my portion;
  therefore I will wait for him."

25 The Lord is good to those whose hope
  is in him, to the one who seeks him;
26 it is good to wait quietly for the
  salvation of the Lord.
27 It is good for a man to bear the yoke
  while he is young.

28 Let him sit alone in silence, for the Lord
  has laid it on him.
29 Let him bury his face in the dust—
  there may yet be hope.
30 Let him offer his cheek to one who
  would strike him, and let him be filled
  with disgrace.

31 For no one is cast off by the Lord forever.
32 Though he brings grief, he will show
  compassion, so great is his unfailing
  love.

33 For he does not willingly bring
    affliction or grief to anyone.

34 To crush underfoot all prisoners in the
    land,
35 to deny people their rights before the
    Most High,
36 to deprive them of justice— would
    not the Lord see such things?

37 Who can speak and have it happen
    if the Lord has not decreed it?
38 Is it not from the mouth of the Most
    High that both calamities and good
    things come?
39 Why should the living complain when
    punished for their sins?

40 Let us examine our ways and test them,
    and let us return to the Lord.
41 Let us lift up our hearts and our hands
    to God in heaven, and say:
42 "We have sinned and rebelled and you
    have not forgiven.

43 "You have covered yourself with anger
    and pursued us; you have slain
    without pity.
44 You have covered yourself with a cloud
    so that no prayer can get through.
45 You have made us scum and refuse
    among the nations.

46 "All our enemies have opened their
    mouths wide against us.

47 We have suffered terror and pitfalls,
    ruin and destruction."
48 Streams of tears flow from my eyes
    because my people are destroyed.

49 My eyes will flow unceasingly, without
    relief,

50 until the Lord looks down from heaven
    and sees.
51 What I see brings grief to my soul
    because of all the women of my city.

52 Those who were my enemies without
    cause hunted me like a bird.
53 They tried to end my life in a pit and
    threw stones at me;
54 the waters closed over my head,
    and I thought I was about to perish.

55 I called on your name, Lord, from the
    depths of the pit.
56 You heard my plea: "Do not close your
    ears to my cry for relief."
57 You came near when I called you,
    and you said, "Do not fear."

58 You, Lord, took up my case; you
    redeemed my life.
59 Lord, you have seen the wrong done to
    me. Uphold my cause!
60 You have seen the depth of their
    vengeance, all their plots against me.

61 Lord, you have heard their insults,
    all their plots against me—
62 what my enemies whisper and mutter
    against me all day long.
63 Look at them! Sitting or standing, they
    mock me in their songs.

64 Pay them back what they deserve, Lord,
    for what their hands have done.
65 Put a veil over their hearts, and may
    your curse be on them!
66 Pursue them in anger and destroy
    them from under the heavens of the
    Lord.

Psalm 30

1 · I will exalt you, LORD,
for you lifted me out of the depths
and did not let my enemies gloat over me.
2 · LORD my God, I called to you for help,
and you healed me.
3 · You, LORD, brought me up from the realm of the dead;
you spared me from going down to the pit.

4 · Sing the praises of the LORD, you his faithful people;
praise his holy name.
5 · For his anger lasts only a moment,
but his favor lasts a lifetime;
weeping may stay for the night,
but rejoicing comes in the morning.

6 · When I felt secure, I said,
"I will never be shaken."
7 · LORD, when you favored me,
you made my royal mountain[c] stand firm;
but when you hid your face,
I was dismayed.

8 · To you, LORD, I called;
to the LORD I cried for mercy:
9 · "What is gained if I am silenced,
if I go down to the pit?
Will the dust praise you?
Will it proclaim your faithfulness?
10 · Hear, LORD, and be merciful to me;
LORD, be my help."

11· You turned my wailing into dancing;
you removed my sackcloth and clothed me with joy,
12 · that my heart may sing your praises and not be silent.
LORD my God, I will praise you forever.

-:- <u>In honor of my dad</u> -:-
who told me I would have a really
good story someday...
If only you knew just how good
a story God had in store.
Thank you for teaching me how
to thrive.

What a joy it is to love someone in
such a grand way that we get to
miss them this much.

Introduction

The prophet Jeremiah wrote Lamentations. To lament means to express grief or sorrow passionately. Jeremiah was lamenting the destruction of Jerusalem by the Babylonians as well as the pain that followed the city and people thereafter. Lamentations 3 is a prayerful song with both expressed pain and praise.

Psalm 30 is a Psalm of David—also a prayerful song like Lamentations 3. However, Psalm 30, in contrast, is filled with predominantly thanksgiving. David had been delivered from his enemies; the Lord had mercy on Him by protecting him from death.

First, I encourage you to read these passages as a whole. To start, Lamentations 3 had a structure that stood out to me. Many people are familiar with the stages of grief:

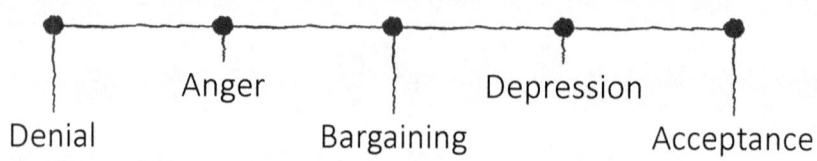

Denial   Anger   Bargaining   Depression   Acceptance

When I lost my dad, I expected this to be the order. A business plan to heal the hurt that came with loss. I would feel these in this exact order, it would all make sense, and then it would be over. I was wrong. The stages looked a little more like this for me:

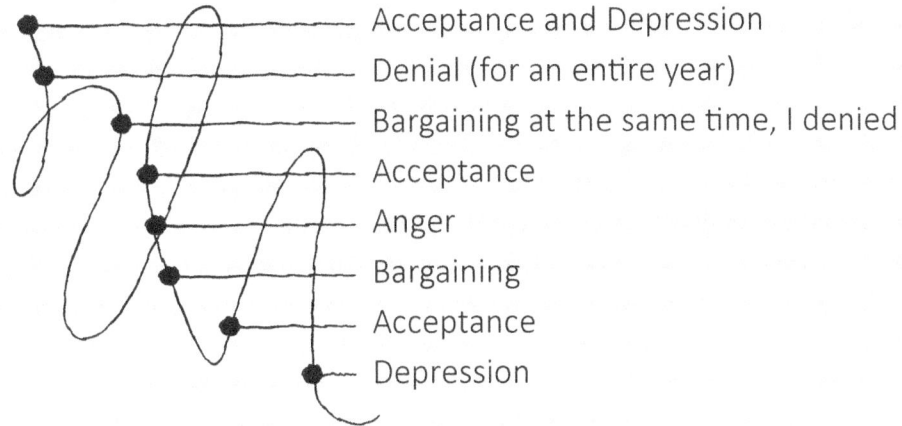

Acceptance and Depression
Denial (for an entire year)
Bargaining at the same time, I denied
Acceptance
Anger
Bargaining
Acceptance
Depression

Bouts of Anger here and there sporadically and simultaneously to other stages. And the cycle continues.

Truth be told, grief never entirely goes away. You don't just stop missing the person you've lost. Grief doesn't go just for death, either. I often think of old friends, and sports I miss. It comes from a lot of things and sticks with us. It comes in waves to be faced every day. That is where the beauty is. The grief doesn't subside. We grow around it. Lamentations 3 starts with pain in Lamentations 3:1-20, but praise soon follows. Afterward, Jeremiah sings more about his pain before praising the Lord again. Like grief and mourning, this passage comes in waves. It comes with pain, praise, and reflection.

<u>Instructions</u> for each page

Pray for Someone Else

Praying for other people has always helped me when I was feeling down. Take some time to write their name and go to war in prayer for them when you are struggling.

Prayer

There is no right or wrong way to pray. It can be as short or long as you'd like. I always just write my thoughts; I write everything I can think of that is on my heart or mind. Sometimes I feel like that gets it out of my head and into the hands of Jesus. Other times when I still have some chaos left in my system, but nothing left to write I will read it to God like a letter. Do what works for you. Your relationship with Christ is different than mine, you are different than me and that is how it should be.

Gratitude Journal

You will always find what you seek. For the gratitude journal pages write out ten things you were grateful for that day. I have also left space for you to write a verse that you are holding on to or another reminder you want to write for yourself. I struggled to come up with ten when I began doing this exercise. On my 100th day I wrote eleven just because I could. It may take time and practice, but I believe in you. Sometimes I write that I am grateful for large and profound things like specific examples of God's provision. Other times I simply write, "coffee." Have at it. There are no rules here.

For your organization, the Gratitude Journal pages are separated in another block *(from page 92)* and should be used along with the other pages.

Free Journaling Pages

These are for whatever you'd like. If you want to write more prayer, go for it. If you want to doodle, go for it. If you just have a lot of feelings and want to scribble the whole page out, go for it. You don't need my permission and this journal is for you. Do whatever helps you and your relationship with Christ. Try new things. Do what you have known to always work for you. Have fun with it.

Bible Study Pages

Take notes about the text you have been encouraged to read. Take note of what stood out to you, and what resonated. Define words that you may not understand or know yet. Read the passage and copy it down to memorize.

There is no right or wrong way to do this as long as you are studying the word of the Lord. Find what works for you to grow closer and more understanding of our great God and go from there. I personally would break down the scripture verse by verse for something like this. I have attached an image of what I would do, but encourage you to make the way you study the Bible personal to you and your relationship with God.

See the example in the next page:

———→

Bible **Study**

Lamentations 3 : 17–20

lacking
something
important

I have been deprived of peace;
I have forgotten what prosperity is.

to prosper is to
thrive & flourish

I have thought
this so many
times before

Then I thought, "My future
is lost, as well as my hope
from the Lord."

pain & suffering

I remember my affliction and
my homelessness, the wormhood
and the poison.

a very bitter plant

I continually remember them
and have become depressed.

Remembering our pain
can become depressing

Wormhood is used here
as a symbol of the
bitterness of hard times

Your journey starts here.

START DATE

END DATE

Bible **Study**

LAMENTATIONS 3:17-20

Devotional

I accepted the loss of my dad in the manner of feeling each emotion that came in the following days. I felt a sense of relief knowing there was no more pain; it was as if someone had lifted a weight off my shoulders on behalf of my dad. I was happy for him, but my heart hurt.

The way these verses were written encapsulates the pain of depression following loss incredibly well. When he died, I felt heavy. I felt like someone knocked the wind out of me, and my heartstrings were attached to my tear ducts a little tighter. If one got tugged, they all were. I even looked dead, in a way. I physically couldn't eat because I had no appetite. In pictures, my skin looked gray, and my smile didn't make it up to my eyes. I was always on the verge of tears. I, like Jeremiah, was deprived of peace and forgot what prosperity was and meant. The splendor and hope were indeed gone. At the time, I only felt the hurt and the lack, but looking back, I remember the loss, bitterness, and broken soul.

Maybe you know this feeling all too well and can remember the days like this. Perhaps you are going through it now. It is okay to feel this way, to have the hurt, no matter what feeling came first or what is to come. Even Jesus grieved, and the people we see as examples of this in the Bible have been here. You are not alone.

Pray for Someone

Prayer

Bible **Study**

Devotional

It was 2018 when my dad died. I did not get saved until 2021. Grief consumed me for nearly three years. I was in too much pain to find it in me to be as kind to others as I should have been. Too calloused to see people's challenges and empathize with them. I couldn't accept what was. I couldn't get enough attention. I never had enough love, or enough people caring about me. My world had crashed down around me. People met me in the rubble for a week, but the wreckage remained long after they left. Their lives went on, and it took years for me to feel like I could keep up. The good news is that your grief doesn't have to look like mine. I didn't have this knowledge of the Lord to call to mind and give me hope. You do!

Every word of the Bible remains true, and the Lord is unchanging. His love is great. With Him and such love, nothing and no one, not even grief, can consume you. He has the unfailing mercy I couldn't bear and never runs out. Every morning, you wake up, and just like verse 23 says, His mercies never end. His faithfulness is great. Your faith in Him can be, too, because you have Christ. The season of mourning is long and seemingly constant. You may not feel God's compassion or faithfulness, and you may not have hope, but the beauty of God is we don't have to see it to believe it. The Lord is enough. He will fill you with the peace that is lost. In due time, you will come out better by God's grace and divine timing. Let Lamentations 3:24-26 be your prayer in this pain. It is well worth the wait.

Pray for Someone

Prayer

Bible **Study**

LAMENTATIONS 3:28-30

Devotional

This season is tough. While you may be praying like I mentioned previously and holding out hope, or at least trying to, it is hard. However, it can be good. It can be a pruning season if you let it.

You will come out different and still good. These verses may sound daunting and harsh. "Let him offer his cheek to one who would strike him; let him be filled with disgrace." is a lot to take in. I am not saying you deserve to be struck and filled with disgrace because you're grief stricken, but I will tell you one thing: This is what it feels like to grieve. You may feel isolated. You may feel like your world has stopped and your life is silent. I remember feeling like I was buried alive, face in the dirt, and being hit by the painful realities of this side of heaven. It hurts.

The depression is real. The denial is real. The anger can be all-consuming. Remember, the Bible is the living word, alive and well. God sees you, hears you, and has written about you. There is better hope to come.

What does your grief feel like?

Be descriptive. Paint an image of it.

How do you feel about your grief?

Are you angry that you're grieving at all?

Do you wish things were different?

What Bible verses can you look to as reminders when these feelings come? Why did you pick these ones?

What are some ways that God could use this for good, even though these circumstances suck?

Are you angry that you're grieving at all?

Do you wish things were different?

Prayer

Bible **Study**

Devotional

The loss of a loved one is not your fault. I, obviously, did not cause my dad's cancer. It doesn't matter if your loss was due to illness, an accident, mental health passing or anything alike, you did not cause it. None of this is your fault. I believe sin is the cause of all things evil, though, and if we as humans could have followed simple directions a long time ago, we would've been well off from the jump, but God knew. God had a plan and wouldn't willingly bring this affliction or grief upon us.

It is a byproduct of all the sin that's ever existed. Luckily, we are wiped clean, made new, and made holy by Christ. Unfortunately, the sacrifice of Jesus does not exempt us from the natural consequence of sin, and we are battling the effects of generations and generations of it.

The good news, though, is that it is a battle already won, but it forces us to find refuge in the One who can protect—the One who can save. We are sure of His promises if we lean in and continue in faithful hope. We will not feel distant and removed forever. He will show compassion because He is a loving, unchanging God. The nature of God, His character, is unwavering and full of unfailing love for you. Yes, He brings grief, and you are going through it right now, but He is with you in the fire. He won the battle before you even knew it existed. He walks before you, beside you, and protects you should you let Him.

Prayer

List off times God has been faithful to you.

Bible **Study**

Devotional

You are hurting. It is okay to say it. The tears are never-ending. When I lost my dad, the slightest things would bring tears to my eyes. They flowed endlessly. Your heart aches if you sit with the grief long enough to feel it pulse through you.

I do not know about you, but thinking of my dad still breaks my heart. Emotions are significant, and to this day, if I embrace the moment of grief, my chest legitimately hurts. Being heartbroken is a reality of loss—a painful, genuine feeling. The world feels like it is after you and hunting you down.

To be truthful, it is. The enemy gets us where it hurts and pokes at the places we are weak. He salts the open wounds. You can't catch a break because it is one thing after another. You get pelted from all angles with difficult things and feel like you can't breathe. It feels like drowning. You can't keep your head above water. What I knew to be my world ended when my dad lost his life. I have been where you are, and so has our guy, Jeremiah. These verses are what grief is. They are what grief feels like. It is real. Again, you are not alone.

Prayer

Bible **Study**

LAMENTATIONS 3:55-57

Devotional

Here, we get to look at Jeremiah as our example. We already know that he gets it. He understands us. I have been through this a handful of times and am glad to be in this space with you. You have gone through the waves of pain with Jeremiah. You know his pain and his revelation. You can call upon the name of the Lord just as Jeremiah does here. I have put a massive emphasis on the fact, yes, the fact, because it is known and proved to be true that God does not change. You can cry out to Him and be honest. Ask Him your questions, grapple with Him, and talk to Him. God is our friend and Father. He will meet you there, and He hears you. Similarly to Jeremiah, our God, compassionate, full of love, good, and faithful, will come to you and tell you not to fear.

You see, God does not promise that everything will be good, and people often get confused by this. "If God is good, why do bad things happen?" We are humans with free will who make bad decisions and face the consequences. Much like I mentioned earlier, we are not only facing the consequences and pain of our sin but also the compounding effects of generations of sin. With sin, bad things happen. Our hope is not that everything will be good. Our hope is that God can use everything for the good of those who love Him. Our good is synonymous with what He provides. It may not look how you planned or wanted it to, but God can use it for His glory. We can find peace and have no fear in knowing that He can use our suffering for good. You may think I'm bananas, but there is joy and delight to be found in suffering for the glory of God, in suffering for the One who suffered for us.

We know that ⌁ **all things**[a] ⌁ work together for **the good**[b] of those who love God, who are called according to his purpose.

a. 8:28 Other mss read that God works together in all things
b. 8:28 The ultimate good

Prayer

Write a Letter to who/what you have lost.

Bible **Study**

PSALM 30:1-5

Devotional

Grief is a lifelong cycle to be lived with and grown around every day. We will live with it for the rest of the time we spend on this side of heaven. That is scary and daunting, but today, I encourage you. The people in the Bible relate and understand. God wrote the Bible for you and me. Our God is so good, He wrote a book for us. Are you kidding me?

Let me tell you this: the closest thing you will ever find to "closure" is peace in Christ. When you experience this, and you will, exalt Him and His name. Elevate Him and sing His praises. It took me years of grief and salvation in Christ to come to this point. Reading Psalm 30, I can attest to every bit of its truth for the grieving heart. It took me nearly four years to call for God's help, and when I did, He healed pieces of me I never thought possible. He spared me from how horrible the trenches are or could have become. The tears still come, and the weeping remains, but Psalm 30:5 acknowledges that.

The good news is not far behind. Rejoicing comes in the morning! Like Lamentations, the waves come, but praise and worship will always follow.

Ways you can praise and worship:

Where do you feel closest to God?

Pray for Someone

Prayer

Bible **Study**

Devotional

This is what I mean when I say grapple with God. Beg Him, plead with Him, ask Him questions, make declarative prayers to Him, and everything in between—no better person to bring it all to than the very One who created it all. You may not see Him, but He is there. He may have hidden His face, but He has not left. You may be distressed and disappointed by how things are going or that He has yet to reveal Himself to you. That is okay. David gets it! I get it! I have tried it my way, and I have tried it God's way. He wants us to go to Him, to talk to Him, and be with Him. I tried the other vices. I tried alcohol, sex, and seeking validation from friends and family. It doesn't work. It never meets the need we so desperately seek to be filled.

You may not see God right now, but I would rather climb mountains to look for Him than ever willingly go back to doing things my way. Seek after God. It is easy to say you will not be shaken when nothing is shaking. It is easy to say you love Jesus when you can tell Jesus loves you. You and I are not perfect, though. There will be days when the world shakes, our lives crumble, and we will doubt. We will be hurt and disappointed, but take heart, my friend. I know of someone you can always go to with absolutely everything. It's the only person who wants you and all your baggage without fail. Take it to the feet of Jesus.

What other vices and idols have you run to when God should have been your first option?

What questions do you have for God?

Prayer

Bible **Study**

Devotional

FOR PSALM 30:11-12

There will be wailing. You know this. There will be heaviness. You know this. Believe it or not, God knew that. Look at what He did for David. The sackcloth was heavy, hot, and uncomfortable as it was worn as an outward show of mourning. You may still cry, but God will take away your wailing so you can show your joy. You may still be heavy sometimes, but God will take the weight and heat so you can be light again. Joy is light. Peace is light.

The day will come. It takes ages sometimes, and you may not think you can bear it. I know I didn't think I could, but I found a friend in Jesus along the way. I asked Him for some help through tears and anger, and we continued to walk the path. He gave me food in the form of fruits of the Spirit. He gave me living water. He gave His life for mine. He provides what I need and discards what I don't. That is just who He is.

When I needed someone to talk to, we talked. When I couldn't walk further, He picked me up and carried me. When I didn't want to move, He sat with me. For David and I, there came a day when we looked at Jesus through bloodshot eyes and with broken hearts. We still carried the weight of our burdens and begged God to be our help.

You know what He did? He wiped our tears, took our bags from us, gave us joy, and said, "Let us dance."
And I know He will do it for you, too.

Prayer

How has Jesus Helped you to joyfully dance lately?

Gratitude Journal

$\longrightarrow$

TRACK YOUR JOURNEY:

DAY 1	DAY 2	DAY 3	DAY 4	DAY 5	DAY 6	DAY 7
DAY 8	DAY 9	DAY 10	DAY 11	DAY 12	DAY 13	DAY 14
DAY 15	DAY 16	DAY 17	DAY 18	DAY 19	DAY 20	DAY 21
DAY 22	DAY 23	DAY 24	DAY 25	DAY 26	DAY 27	DAY 28
DAY 29	DAY 30	DAY 31	DAY 32	DAY 33	DAY 34	DAY 35
DAY 36	DAY 37	DAY 38	DAY 39	DAY 40	DAY 41	DAY 42
DAY 43	DAY 44	DAY 45	DAY 46	DAY 47	DAY 48	DAY 49
DAY 50	DAY 51	DAY 52	DAY 53	DAY 54	DAY 55	DAY 56

Gratitude Journal

1.

2.

3.

4.

5.

6.

7.

8.

9.

10.

VERSE/REMINDER: _____

_____

_____

Gratitude Journal

1 ·

2 ·

3 ·

4 ·

5 ·

6 ·

7 ·

8 ·

9 ·

10 ·

VERSE/REMINDER: _____

_____

_____

Gratitude Journal

1.

2.

3.

4.

5.

6.

7.

8.

9.

10.

VERSE/REMINDER: _____

_____

_____

Gratitude Journal

1 ·

2 ·

3 ·

4 ·

5 ·

6 ·

7 ·

8 ·

9 ·

10 ·

VERSE/REMINDER: _____
_____
_____

Gratitude Journal

1 .

2 .

3 .

4 .

5 .

6 .

7 .

8 .

9 .

10 .

VERSE/REMINDER: _____

_____

_____

Gratitude Journal

1 .

2 .

3 .

4 .

5 .

6 .

7 .

8 .

9 .

10 .

VERSE/REMINDER: _____

_____

_____

Gratitude Journal

1.

2.

3.

4.

5.

6.

7.

8.

9.

10.

VERSE/REMINDER: _____

_____

Gratitude Journal

1.

2.

3.

4.

5.

6.

7.

8.

9.

10.

VERSE/REMINDER: _____

_____

_____

Gratitude Journal

1.

2.

3.

4.

5.

6.

7.

8.

9.

10.

VERSE/REMINDER: _____

_____

_____

Gratitude Journal

1 ·

2 ·

3 ·

4 ·

5 ·

6 ·

7 ·

8 ·

9 ·

10 ·

VERSE/REMINDER: _____

_____

_____

Gratitude Journal

1.

2.

3.

4.

5.

6.

7.

8.

9.

10.

VERSE/REMINDER: _____

_____

_____

Gratitude Journal

1 .

2 .

3 .

4 .

5 .

6 .

7 .

8 .

9 .

10 .

VERSE/REMINDER: _____

_____

_____

Gratitude Journal

1.

2.

3.

4.

5.

6.

7.

8.

9.

10.

VERSE/REMINDER: _____

_____

_____

Gratitude Journal

1 .

2 .

3 .

4 .

5 .

6 .

7 .

8 .

9 .

10 .

VERSE/REMINDER: _____

_____

_____

Gratitude Journal

1.

2.

3.

4.

5.

6.

7.

8.

9.

10.

VERSE/REMINDER: _____

_____

_____

Gratitude Journal

1.

2.

3.

4.

5.

6.

7.

8.

9.

10.

VERSE/REMINDER: _____

_____

_____

Gratitude Journal

1.

2.

3.

4.

5.

6.

7.

8.

9.

10.

VERSE/REMINDER:

Gratitude Journal

1.

2.

3.

4.

5.

6.

7.

8.

9.

10.

VERSE/REMINDER: _____

_____

_____

Gratitude Journal

1.

2.

3.

4.

5.

6.

7.

8.

9.

10.

VERSE/REMINDER: _____

_____

_____

Gratitude Journal

1.

2.

3.

4.

5.

6.

7.

8.

9.

10.

VERSE/REMINDER: _____

_____

_____

Gratitude Journal

1.

2.

3.

4.

5.

6.

7.

8.

9.

10.

VERSE/REMINDER: _____

_____

_____

Gratitude Journal

1 ·

2 ·

3 ·

4 ·

5 ·

6 ·

7 ·

8 ·

9 ·

10 ·

VERSE/REMINDER: _____
_____
_____

Gratitude Journal

1.

2.

3.

4.

5.

6.

7.

8.

9.

10.

VERSE/REMINDER: _____

_____

_____

Gratitude Journal

1.

2.

3.

4.

5.

6.

7.

8.

9.

10.

VERSE/REMINDER: _____

_____

_____

Gratitude Journal

1.

2.

3.

4.

5.

6.

7.

8.

9.

10.

VERSE/REMINDER: _____

_____

_____

Gratitude Journal

1.

2.

3.

4.

5.

6.

7.

8.

9.

10.

VERSE/REMINDER: _____

_____

_____

Gratitude Journal

1.

2.

3.

4.

5.

6.

7.

8.

9.

10.

VERSE/REMINDER: _____

_____

_____

Gratitude Journal

1 .

2 .

3 .

4 .

5 .

6 .

7 .

8 .

9 .

10 .

VERSE/REMINDER: _____

_____

_____

Gratitude Journal

1.

2.

3.

4.

5.

6.

7.

8.

9.

10.

VERSE/REMINDER: _____

_____

_____

Gratitude Journal

1 .

2 .

3 .

4 .

5 .

6 .

7 .

8 .

9 .

10 .

VERSE/REMINDER: _____

_____

_____

Gratitude Journal

1.

2.

3.

4.

5.

6.

7.

8.

9.

10.

VERSE/REMINDER: _____

_____

_____

Gratitude Journal

1.

2.

3.

4.

5.

6.

7.

8.

9.

10.

VERSE/REMINDER: _____

_____

_____

Gratitude Journal

1 ·

2 ·

3 ·

4 ·

5 ·

6 ·

7 ·

8 ·

9 ·

10 ·

VERSE/REMINDER: _____

_____

_____

Gratitude Journal

1 .

2 .

3 .

4 .

5 .

6 .

7 .

8 .

9 .

10 .

VERSE/REMINDER: _____

_____

_____

Gratitude Journal

1.

2.

3.

4.

5.

6.

7.

8.

9.

10.

VERSE/REMINDER: _____

_____

_____

Gratitude Journal

1.

2.

3.

4.

5.

6.

7.

8.

9.

10.

VERSE/REMINDER: _____

_____

_____

Gratitude Journal

1.

2.

3.

4.

5.

6.

7.

8.

9.

10.

VERSE/REMINDER: _____

_____

_____

Gratitude Journal

1.

2.

3.

4.

5.

6.

7.

8.

9.

10.

VERSE/REMINDER: _____

_____

_____

Gratitude Journal

1.

2.

3.

4.

5.

6.

7.

8.

9.

10.

VERSE/REMINDER: _____

_____

_____

Gratitude Journal

1 .

2 .

3 .

4 .

5 .

6 .

7 .

8 .

9 .

10 .

VERSE/REMINDER: _____

_____

_____

Gratitude Journal

1.

2.

3.

4.

5.

6.

7.

8.

9.

10.

VERSE/REMINDER: _____

_____

_____

Gratitude Journal

1 .

2 .

3 .

4 .

5 .

6 .

7 .

8 .

9 .

10 .

VERSE/REMINDER: _____

_____

_____

Gratitude Journal

1.

2.

3.

4.

5.

6.

7.

8.

9.

10.

VERSE/REMINDER: _____

_____

_____

Gratitude Journal

1.

2.

3.

4.

5.

6.

7.

8.

9.

10.

VERSE/REMINDER: _____

_____

_____

Gratitude Journal

1.

2.

3.

4.

5.

6.

7.

8.

9.

10.

VERSE/REMINDER: _____

_____

_____

Gratitude Journal

1 .

2 .

3 .

4 .

5 .

6 .

7 .

8 .

9 .

10 .

VERSE/REMINDER: _____

_____

_____

Gratitude Journal

1 ·

2 ·

3 ·

4 ·

5 ·

6 ·

7 ·

8 ·

9 ·

10 ·

VERSE/REMINDER: _____

_____

_____

Gratitude Journal

1 .

2 .

3 .

4 .

5 .

6 .

7 .

8 .

9 .

10 .

VERSE/REMINDER: _____

_____

_____

Gratitude Journal

1.

2.

3.

4.

5.

6.

7.

8.

9.

10.

VERSE/REMINDER: _____

_____

_____

Gratitude Journal

1 .

2 .

3 .

4 .

5 .

6 .

7 .

8 .

9 .

10 .

VERSE/REMINDER: _____

_____

_____

Gratitude Journal

1.

2.

3.

4.

5.

6.

7.

8.

9.

10.

VERSE/REMINDER: _____

_____

_____

Gratitude Journal

1 .

2 .

3 .

4 .

5 .

6 .

7 .

8 .

9 .

10 .

VERSE/REMINDER: _____

_____

_____

Gratitude Journal

1.

2.

3.

4.

5.

6.

7.

8.

9.

10.

VERSE/REMINDER: _____

_____

_____

Gratitude Journal

1 .

2 .

3 .

4 .

5 .

6 .

7 .

8 .

9 .

10 .

VERSE/REMINDER: _____

_____

_____

Gratitude Journal

1.

2.

3.

4.

5.

6.

7.

8.

9.

10.

VERSE/REMINDER: _____

_____

Gratitude Journal

1 .

2 .

3 .

4 .

5 .

6 .

7 .

8 .

9 .

10 .

VERSE/REMINDER: _____

_____

_____

Let me **leave you** with this...

My prayer is that no matter what, when or how, you will give Him all the glory. Here is my advice, praise Him in the highs, lows and even when it hurts. I assure you, it is the best choice you will ever make.

About the **Author**

If you were to ask me the top three things that made me who I am today, I would say doing gymnastics for thirteen years, losing my dad to cancer, and sorority recruitment. I know this sounds ridiculous, and I won't go into depth today, but I will tell you one thing they have in common: God worked them all together to lead me straight to Him. He has blessed me with the ability and resources to be a first-time author with this journal, a student pursuing a Bachelor's degree in Marketing at Oklahoma State University, a friend to the best people you could meet, a daughter to the most incredible parents in the whole wide world, a sister to siblings who never fail to make me laugh, and most importantly a daughter to the Most High.

Thank you for allowing me to embark on this journey with grief alongside you. It is a bittersweet gift.

With love,
Veronica Turner
@veronicaturner_